the Living Ocean
Skates and Rays

Rebecca Sjonger & Bobbie Kalman

🍄 Crabtree Publishing Company

www.crabtreebooks.com

the Living Ocean

Created by Bobbie Kalman

Dedicated by Margaret Amy Salter
To Andrew, Lauren, and Eric
Three "rays" of sunshine that came "skating" into my life.

Editor-in-Chief
Bobbie Kalman

Writing team
Rebecca Sjonger
Bobbie Kalman

Substantive editor
Kelley MacAulay

Editors
Molly Aloian
Robin Johnson
Reagan Miller
Kathryn Smithyman

Design
Margaret Amy Salter
Samantha Crabtree (cover)

Production coordinator
Heather Fitzpatrick

Photo research
Crystal Foxton

Consultant
Patricia Loesche, Ph.D., Animal Behavior Program,
Department of Psychology, University of Washington

Illustrations
Barbara Bedell: pages 5 (angel shark), 26-27 (shark and shrimp)
Katherine Kantor: pages 4, 5 (skate)
Cori Marvin: page 5 (ray)
Bonna Rouse: pages 5 (ratfish and guitarfish), 6, 7, 11, 20 (mackerels),
   26-27 (stingray and skate), 29
Margaret Amy Salter: pages 20 (crab and marine worms), 26-27 (all except
   stingray, shark, shrimp, and skate)

Photographs
Bobbie Kalman: page 3
© Georgette Douwma/naturepl.com: front cover
Jeffery Rotman Photography: Jeff Rotman: page 19
SeaPics.com: Shedd Aquar/Ceisel: page 10; Shedd Aquar/Lines Jr.: page 8 (top);
   Jonathan Bird: page 18; Jeff Jaskolski: page 20; Andrew J. Martinez: page 15;
   Jeff Rotman: pages 9 (bottom), 16 (top), 21 (top); Mark Strickland: page 13;
   Lin Sutherland: page 23
Other images by Corel, Digital Vision, and Digital Stock

Crabtree Publishing Company

www.crabtreebooks.com   1-800-387-7650

Cataloging-in-Publication Data
Sjonger, Rebecca.
   Skates and rays / Rebecca Sjonger & Bobbie Kalman.
      p. cm. -- (The living ocean series)
   ISBN-13: 978-0-7787-1303-6 (rlb)
   ISBN-10: 0-7787-1303-2 (rlb)
   ISBN-13: 978-0-7787-1325-8 (pbk)
   ISBN-10: 0-7787-1325-3 (pbk)
   1. Skates (Fishes)--Juvenile literature. 2. Rays (Fishes)--Juvenile literature.
   I. Kalman, Bobbie. II. Title. III. Series.
   QL638.85.R3S56 2006
   597.3'5--dc22
                                                    2005019992
                                                    LC

**Published in
the United States**
PMB16A
350 Fifth Ave.
Suite 3308
New York, NY
10118

**Published
in Canada**
616 Welland Ave.,
St. Catharines, Ontario
Canada
L2M 5V6

**Published in the
United Kingdom**
73 Lime Walk
Headington
Oxford
OX3 7AD
United Kingdom

**Published
in Australia**
386 Mt. Alexander Rd.,
Ascot Vale (Melbourne)
VIC 3032

Contents

What are skates and rays?

Skates and rays are fish. Fish are **vertebrates**. Vertebrates are animals with backbones. Like all fish, skates and rays breathe by taking in **oxygen** from the water. They breathe using body parts called **gills**. Most fish, including skates and rays, are **cold-blooded** animals. The body temperatures of cold-blooded animals change as the temperatures of their surroundings change.

Skates and rays, such as this blue-spotted stingray, have flat bodies. Their flat bodies make them look different from other kinds of fish.

Cartilaginous fish

Skates and rays belong to a group of fish called **cartilaginous fish**. Cartilaginous fish have skeletons made of **cartilage**. Cartilage is a tough, bendable material. The material in your ears is cartilage. Cartilage is lighter than bone. Other cartilaginous fish include ratfish, guitarfish, sharks, chimaeras, and sawfish. Skates and rays are closely related to sawfish, guitarfish, and sharks.

ratfish

The bodies of ratfish are longer and narrower than the bodies of skates and rays are.

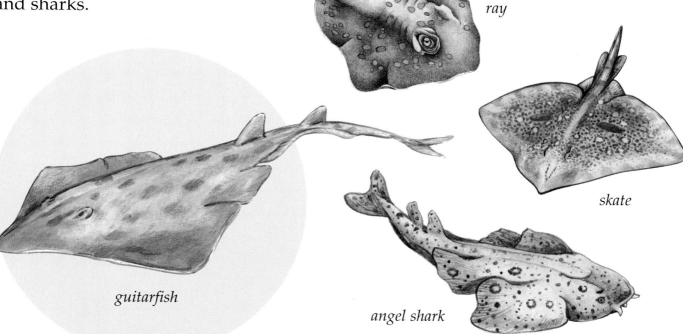

ray

skate

guitarfish

angel shark

Guitarfish, sawfish, skates, rays, and sharks all have similar body parts.

A few types of sharks, such as angel sharks, have flat bodies that are similar to the bodies of skates and rays.

Spectacular species

There are hundreds of **species**, or types, of skates and rays. Scientists believe that there are many more species yet to be discovered. Different species of skates and rays have bodies that are different sizes, shapes, and colors. These pages show some species of skates and rays.

The longnose skate has a long, pointed snout!

The bull's-eye electric ray has a pattern on its back that looks like a round target called a "bull's-eye."

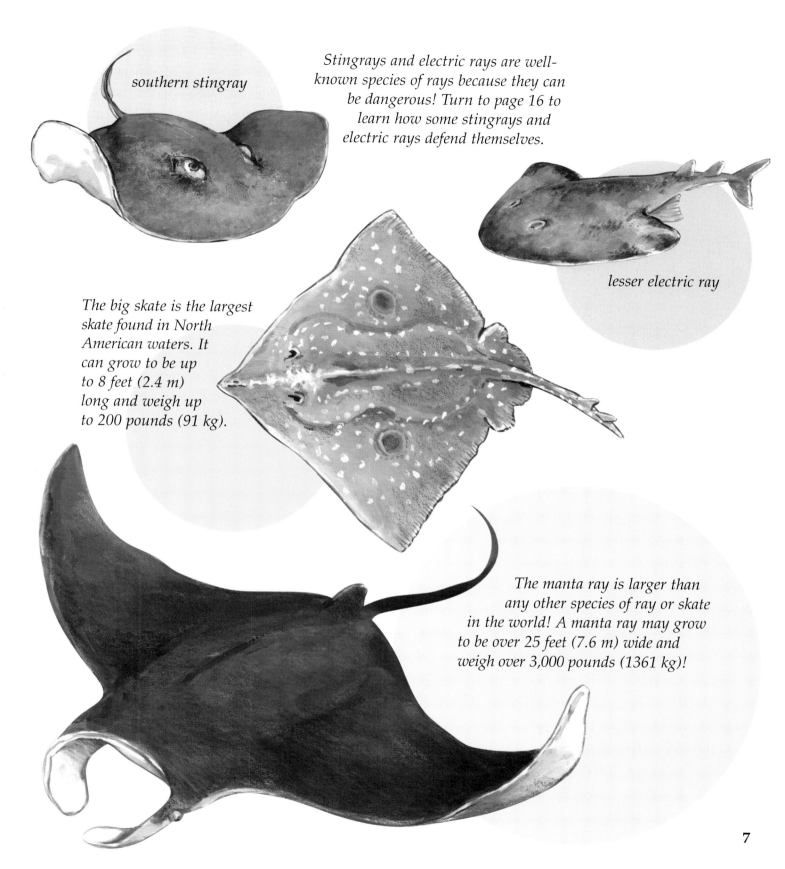

southern stingray

Stingrays and electric rays are well-known species of rays because they can be dangerous! Turn to page 16 to learn how some stingrays and electric rays defend themselves.

lesser electric ray

The big skate is the largest skate found in North American waters. It can grow to be up to 8 feet (2.4 m) long and weigh up to 200 pounds (91 kg).

The manta ray is larger than any other species of ray or skate in the world! A manta ray may grow to be over 25 feet (7.6 m) wide and weigh over 3,000 pounds (1361 kg)!

*Ocellate river stingrays live in warm freshwater rivers in the Amazon **rain forest**.*

Skates and rays live in different **habitats**. A habitat is the natural place where an animal lives. Most skates and rays live in saltwater habitats, such as oceans and seas. Other skates and rays live in freshwater habitats, such as lakes and rivers. Some species also live in **estuaries**. An estuary is a body of water that is formed when a river meets an ocean. In estuaries, salt water and fresh water mix together. Most skates and rays live in habitats where the water is warm, but some of these fish live in **polar** habitats, where the water is cold.

Different depths

Different species of skates and rays live in waters of different depths. Most skates and rays are **bottom dwellers**. Bottom dwellers live near or on the bottom of bodies of water. They often live in waters with sandy or muddy bottoms. Bottom-dwelling skates and rays may live as deep as 10,000 feet (3048 m) beneath the ocean's surface! Other skates and rays swim in shallow waters. They live close to the surface. Many species of skates and rays swim to other depths when they look for food, however.

The thornback skate is a bottom dweller.

Near or far from shore?

Some skates and rays live in ocean waters near shores. They may live around **coral reefs** or in areas where **kelp**, or seaweed, grows. Other skates and rays live far from shores in open oceans. Some species move throughout open ocean waters, whereas others live on the bottom of open oceans.

Living alone

Some species of skates and rays are **solitary**. Solitary animals do not live with other animals. Solitary fish, including skates and rays, gather with other fish only when it is time to **mate**.

Swimming in schools

Some species of skates and rays live in groups called **schools**. A few species of skates and rays are solitary most of the time, but they live in schools when there is plenty of food. Bat rays, for example, are mainly solitary, but thousands of them have been seen together in places where there is plenty of food.

Manta rays move through open ocean waters. They spend more time swimming than bottom dwellers do.

Cownose rays live in schools.

9

Body basics

Skates and rays have many body parts in common with all fish. For example, every skate and ray has eyes, a mouth, gills, fins, and a tail. The bodies of skates and rays are called **disks** because they are wide and flat in shape. Having disk-shaped bodies helps skates and rays move easily through water. The body of a skate and that of a ray look so similar that it can be difficult to tell them apart. These pages show some of the similarities and differences between skates and rays.

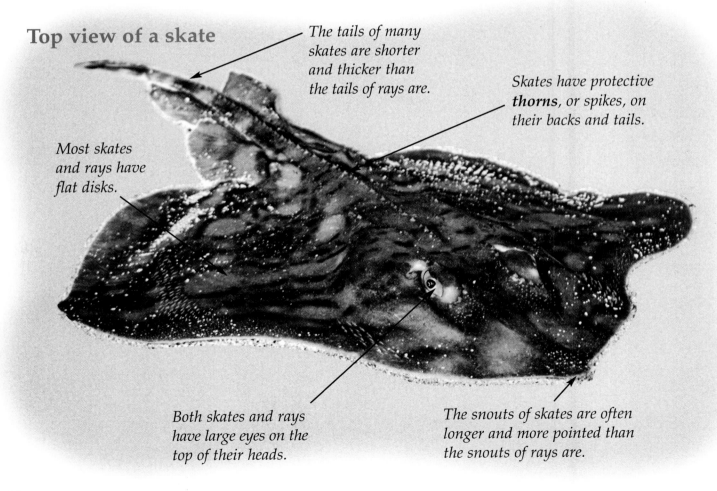

Top view of a skate

The tails of many skates are shorter and thicker than the tails of rays are.

*Skates have protective **thorns**, or spikes, on their backs and tails.*

Most skates and rays have flat disks.

Both skates and rays have large eyes on the top of their heads.

The snouts of skates are often longer and more pointed than the snouts of rays are.

Breathing on the bottom

Skates and rays breathe by taking in oxygen from water. First, they draw water into their **spiracles**, which are holes behind their eyes. After water enters the spiracles, it passes through the gills. The gills take oxygen from the water and pass it into the blood of the animals. Skates and rays then push the water out of their bodies through **gill slits**, which are located on the undersides of their disks.

stingray spiracle

Bottom view of a ray

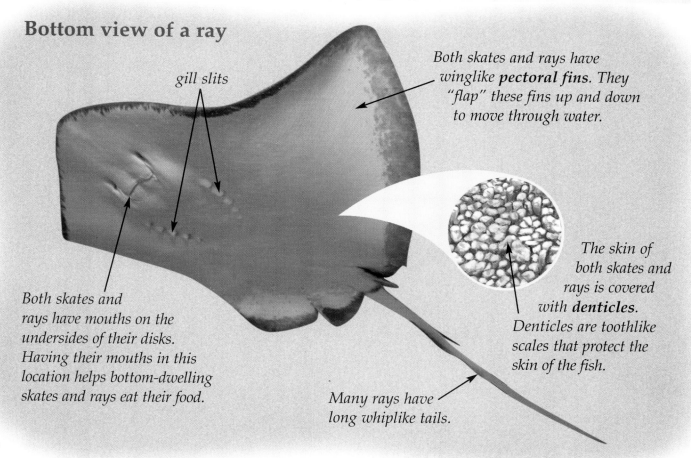

gill slits

*Both skates and rays have winglike **pectoral fins**. They "flap" these fins up and down to move through water.*

Both skates and rays have mouths on the undersides of their disks. Having their mouths in this location helps bottom-dwelling skates and rays eat their food.

Many rays have long whiplike tails.

*The skin of both skates and rays is covered with **denticles**. Denticles are toothlike scales that protect the skin of the fish.*

11

In the water

Skates and rays swim easily through water. They swim by "flapping" their winglike pectoral fins. Skates and rays flap their fins, just as birds flap their wings. They move them up and down to push their bodies forward. Skates and rays do not sink because they have oil-filled **organs** called livers in their bodies. Oil is lighter than water. The oil in the livers of skates and rays makes the bodies of these fish light and helps them stay afloat.

Taking a walk

Most fish move by swimming, but some bottom-dwelling skates can "walk!" These skates can move along the ocean floor using body parts called **crura**. Crura, which are like tiny legs, are attached to the **pelvic fins** of the skates. The skates use their crura to push their bodies off the bottom of oceans. After they glide forward and land, the skates push themselves off again.

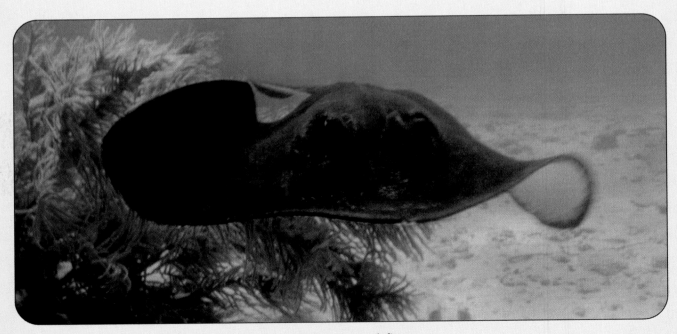

Skates and rays also stay afloat by moving their pectoral fins.

Skates and rays seem to fly through the water when they swim. These southern stingrays are moving by flapping their large pectoral fins.

Super senses

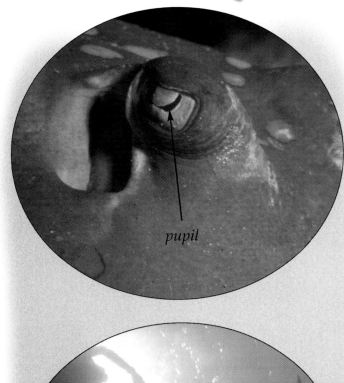

pupil

Skates and rays have several ways of sensing their surroundings. One of the most helpful senses these fish have is good vision. Having eyes at the top of their heads allows skates and rays to spot nearby fish and other animals above and around them. The eyes of skates and rays have narrow **pupils**. Having narrow pupils allows these fish to see clearly the movements of other animals. Layers of **tissue** over their eyes also filter out the glare of bright sunlight sparkling through water.

Good vibrations

Skates and rays also have **lateral lines** to help them sense their surroundings. Lateral lines are rows of fluid-filled tubes on the undersides of skates and rays. When another animal swims near a skate or a ray, that animal's movements create tiny ripples in the water, which are called **vibrations**. A skate or ray feels these vibrations with its lateral lines and can sense that another animal is nearby.

The movements of these divers create vibrations in the water. The manta ray feels the vibrations with its lateral lines.

Charge!

All living things give off weak electrical charges. Skates and rays have body parts called **ampullae of Lorenzini**. These parts sense the electrical charges given off by the other living things in the ocean. The ampullae of Lorenzini are located in the head of a skate or a ray. Studies show that some species of skates and rays are most sensitive to the charges given off by their **predators**. Predators are animals that hunt and eat other animals. The ampullae of Lorenzini also help skates and rays find **prey**, or animals that they hunt and eat.

Sending shocks

In addition to sensing electrical charges, some species of skates and rays also create charges. Some skates, such as the winter skate shown below, produce harmless electrical charges with organs that are located along the sides of their tails. These electrical charges help other skates identify the species or the sex of the skate that sent the charges. Electric rays have organs that can produce harmful electrical charges. The rays use these charges to protect themselves from other animals. For more information on the defenses used by electric rays, turn to page 16.

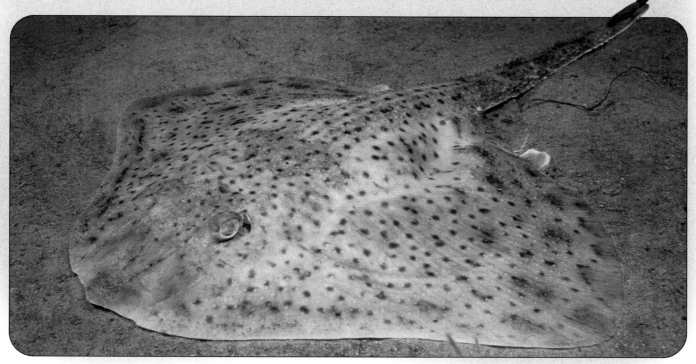

Skate and ray defenses

Most skates and rays are slow-moving animals that are at risk of being eaten by speedier predators. To protect themselves, some species of skates and rays have body parts that discourage predators from getting too close. Some skate species have hooked thorns along their backs or on the edges of their disks. Some ray species have **spines**, or sharp points, along their backs or tails. The spines of some ray species are especially dangerous. Stingrays, bat rays, and eagle rays all have one or more spines that contain poison.

a ray's tail spine

Armed and dangerous!

Electric rays have two organs in their disks that produce powerful electric shocks. They use these shocks to protect themselves from predators. When an electric ray senses danger, it quickly creates a charge of electricity that surrounds its body. Electric rays are very dangerous, so few other animals try to attack them! The Atlantic torpedo ray, shown right, is an electric ray.

Camouflage

Most skates and rays have **camouflaged** disks. Camouflaged animals have colors and patterns that help hide the animals in their natural surroundings. Most bottom-dwelling skates and rays are camouflaged on the upper sides of their disks. The skin on their upper sides is often sandy-brown in color. It may be marked with spots that blend in with stones on the ocean floor. A predator swimming above a camouflaged skate or ray cannot tell the difference between the animal's disk and the ocean floor. Bottom-dwelling skates and rays do not need camouflage on the lower sides of their disks, since their predators only see them from above.

This blue-spotted lagoon ray has markings on its body that look like stones on the ocean floor.

Countershading

Skates and rays that swim near the surface of oceans need camouflage on both sides of their disks. These skates and rays often have a type of camouflage called **countershading**. Animals with countershading have dark backs and light bellies. When a predator swims above a skate or ray, it may not see the fish because its dark back blends in with the dark ocean floor. When a predator swims below the skate or ray, it may not see the fish because its light belly blends in with the sunlit surface waters.

The body of this southern stingray has countershading.

17

Baby skates

Mature, or adult, skates are able to mate and make babies. At least once each year, male skates search for female skates with which to mate. After a male and a female have mated, the female lays flat, rectangular **egg cases**. Each egg case holds an egg. Most skates lay two or more egg cases at a time. Some skate species lay egg cases that have stemlike parts. These parts anchor the egg cases to underwater plants.

A skate is born

Depending on its species, a baby skate **gestates**, or develops inside its egg case, for two to eighteen months. There is a **yolk** inside the egg case, which the baby eats. The baby grows inside its egg case until it is large enough to **hatch**. The baby skate, shown above, is hatching from its egg case. The newly hatched skate looks like a small adult skate. The baby skate takes care of itself after hatching.

Baby rays

Baby rays develop differently than baby skates do. After male and female rays mate, the female rays do not lay egg cases. Instead, mother rays keep their egg cases inside their bodies. The babies are safe from predators inside the bodies of their mothers. The larger the female ray is, the longer her babies take to develop inside her body. Different species of female rays carry different numbers of egg cases.

Tail-first delivery

When a baby ray is fully developed, it hatches from its egg case. It then leaves its mother's body tailfirst, as shown above. The dangerous parts of the baby's body, such as sharp spines, are usually covered in tissue to keep them from harming the mother. Baby rays take care of themselves immediately. They must find their own food and avoid predators.

Feeding habits

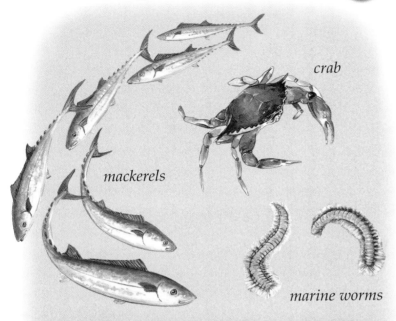

crab

mackerels

marine worms

Most skates and rays are **carnivores**. Carnivores are animals that eat other animals. Different species of skates and rays eat different kinds of animals. Many skates and rays eat fish, **crustaceans**, and marine worms.

Fish foods

Skates and rays eat the foods that are available in their habitats. For example, the skates and rays that live on the ocean floor are surrounded by many kinds of **mollusks**. Mollusks are animals with hard shells and soft bodies. Skates and rays that live in shallow coastal waters eat mainly different species of crustaceans. Those that live in open oceans eat foods that float in water, such as **plankton**. Plankton are **microscopic** plants and animals.

This southern stingray has trapped a fish beneath its disk.

Tough teeth

Many skates and rays have hard, round teeth. Their teeth are made of a strong material that is similar to bone. Skates and rays use their hard teeth to crush the shells of prey animals, such as crabs and clams. Once a shell is cracked open, the skate or ray eats the soft body of the animal inside.

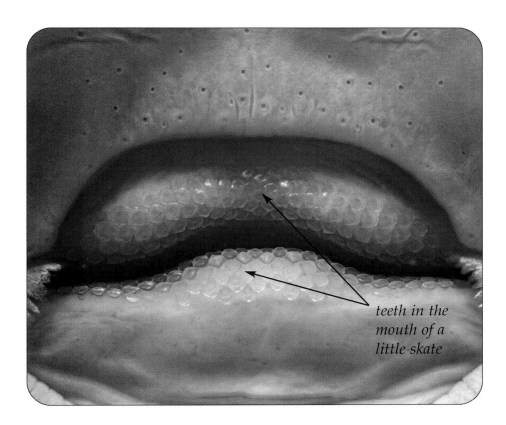

teeth in the mouth of a little skate

Microscopic meals

Manta rays and a few other species of skates and rays are **filter feeders**. Filter feeders eat by swimming with their mouths open and **filtering**, or straining, food from the water. A manta ray uses the fins on its head to pull food such as plankton into its mouth, as shown right. The manta ray has parts in its mouth that filter plankton from the water. The filtered water leaves the ray's body through its gills.

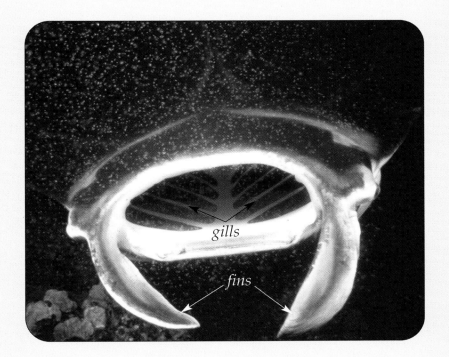

gills

fins

Finding food

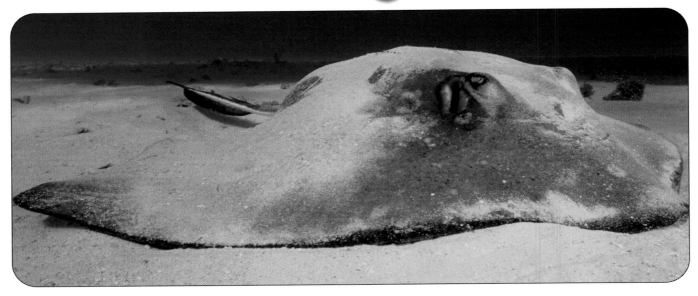

Different skates and rays have different ways of catching prey. Some bottom-dwelling skates and rays seek out prey that are buried beneath sand. A skate or ray may find the prey by blowing streams of water from its mouth. The water blasts through mud and sand, revealing the hidden animal. When the prey is revealed, the skate or ray presses its disk down onto the prey and then quickly pulls its disk up again. This motion creates suction, which pulls the prey from beneath the sand. When the prey is out of the sand, the skate or ray sucks it into its mouth and eats it.

What a flop!

Some bottom-dwelling skates and rays hunt by staying still. Their camouflaged skin is often the same color or pattern as that of the sandy or muddy ocean floor on which they live. If a bottom dweller lies still, prey animals may not notice it until they have come very close, and by then it is too late! The hungry skate or ray flops its disk on top of the unsuspecting prey. The skate or ray then eats the trapped prey.

This southern stingray is hiding under some sand. When a prey animal comes close, the stingray attacks the animal.

Sneaky somersaults

Manta rays perform somersaults to gather food! When a manta ray finds a food source, such as a cluster of plankton floating in the ocean, it swims in slow, wide somersaults through the plankton. The movement of the water creates suction, which draws the plankton toward the manta ray. The filter-feeding manta ray then uses its fins to push the food toward its open mouth.

What a shock!

Electric rays sometimes use their electricity-producing body parts to catch prey. When a fish such as a halibut or a salmon swims by, an electric ray quickly shocks its prey. The electric ray then brings the stunned fish to its mouth. The shocks of some electric rays are strong enough to break the backbones of their prey!

The manta ray, shown above, is somersaulting through plankton.

Balanced ecosystems

Skates and rays belong to communities of living things that are connected to one another and to the surroundings in which they live. These communities are called **ecosystems**. An ecosystem is made up of plants, animals, and non-living natural things. Ecosystems that include skates and rays are found in coral reefs, in estuaries, and in many other underwater habitats. Even the slightest change to any part of the community that makes up an ecosystem may cause that ecosystem to become unbalanced and unhealthy.

Diverse ecosystems

One way scientists measure the overall health of an ecosystem is by looking at its **biological diversity**. Biological diversity means the variety and number of plants and animals that live in the ecosystem. A wide variety of food sources and plenty of sunshine create ecosystems with the most biological diversity. Tropical ecosystems, found near the **equator**, have the greatest biological diversity. Many species of skates and rays, as well as many other plants and animals, live in tropical ecosystems.

Food chains and webs

Plants and animals in an ecosystem need food to get the energy they need to survive. Plants can make their own food. Animals, however, must eat plants and other animals to stay alive. The pattern of eating and being eaten is called a **food chain**. In a food chain, energy is passed from one animal to the next. When an animal from one food chain eats an animal from another food chain, the food chains become connected. Two or more connecting food chains form a **food web**.

A healthy balance

An animal at the top of a food chain is called an **apex predator**. Apex predators that eat skates and rays include sharks and whales. By hunting, apex predators help keep food webs and ecosystems stable and balanced. For example, if the **population** of stingrays grew too large, hammerhead sharks would hunt more of them, bringing the number of stingrays back to normal. If the sharks did not control the stingray populations, the number of stingrays would increase. The amount of food available to the rays would stay the same, so there would not be enough food to feed all the stingrays. When the lives of skates and rays are threatened, their predators, prey, and even the ecosystem to which they belong are also in danger.

Apex predators, such as this hammerhead shark, are important animals in food chains and webs.

A food web

Skates and rays are important parts of the food chains and webs in their habitats. A food web that includes skates and rays is shown on these pages. The arrows in the food web point toward the living things that are receiving energy. For example, the web shows that blue crabs eat marine worms and that southern stingrays eat blue crabs. The variety of animals in this web shows that the web is healthy. Follow the arrows to see how different food chains join together to form a food web.

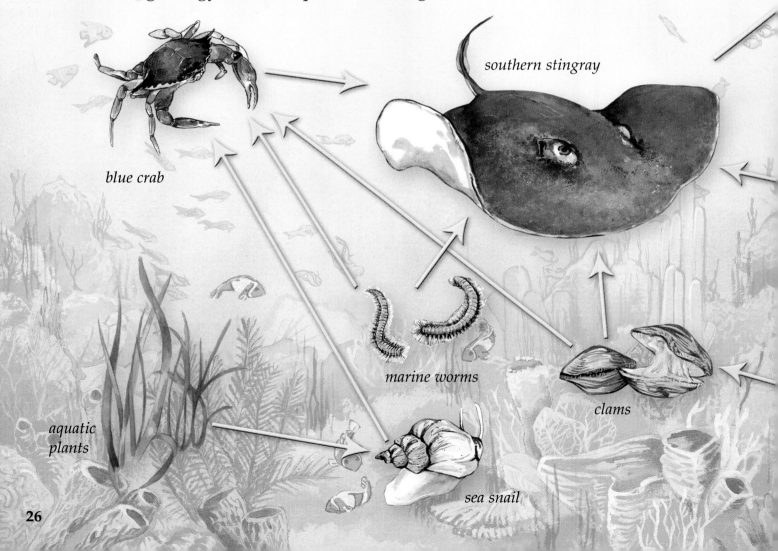

southern stingray

blue crab

marine worms

clams

aquatic plants

sea snail

hammerhead shark

big skate

shrimp

clams

marine worms

plankton

lobster

27

Fish in danger!

Most underwater habitats are threatened. The greatest dangers to the habitats and the animals that live in them are the result of human activities, especially fishing. Large-bodied skates and rays are popular catches with **fisheries** that sell them for meat. In some places, these skates and rays are **overfished**. Overfishing occurs when fishers take too many species of fish from an area. Some fishers accidentally take skates and rays from the water as **bycatch**. Bycatch are animals that are trapped in huge nets, which are meant to catch other underwater animals. Some fishers use the skates and rays they catch as bait to catch other fish. Many other fishers simply throw away the unwanted skates and rays as garbage.

Skates and rays are often caught in huge nets that are meant to catch other species of fish.

Polluted habitats

Environmental damage caused by pollution also harms skates and rays. The waters in which the fish live are being polluted by chemicals and garbage produced by factories, towns, and cities. The habitats in which skates and rays live can become so damaged, that living things can no longer survive in them.

Slow-motion reproduction

Most species of skates and rays take several years to mature and make babies. When they do have babies, they have fewer than most other fish have. As a result, the populations of skate-and-ray species grow slowly. If too many skates and rays are harmed by human activities, there may not be enough babies to replace the fish that are killed.

Pollution, such as the chemicals shown above, washes into rivers and streams. It eventually ends up in oceans.

Endangered species

Some species of skates and rays, such as spotback skates and pincushion rays, are **endangered**. Scientists believe that there are still undiscovered species of skates and rays that may die out before they can be found and studied. To learn more about endangered skates and rays, as well as many other animals, visit the IUCN Red List of Threatened Species website online at www.redlist.org.

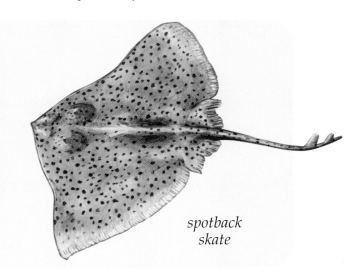

spotback skate

Skates, rays, and you

Long ago, sailors caught skates and rays, let their bodies dry, and then twisted their bodies into frightening figures. When people saw these creations, they believed the sailors had captured sea monsters! People today know that skates and rays are not frightening monsters. The only time these fish attack humans is when they are defending themselves.

Out of the wild

The wide variety of underwater habitats in which skates and rays live makes it difficult for scientists to study these animals. For this reason, some skates and rays are placed in aquariums, where they can be watched more closely. Aquariums are not ideal homes for skates and rays, however. If you visit an aquarium that has skates and rays, remember that their tanks are much different than the natural places in which skates and rays usually live.

Swimmers and divers should never try to touch skates or rays, as the diver shown above is doing! If people leave skates and rays alone, both the people and the animals will remain safe from harm.

Learn more

There are hundreds of species of skates and rays. Each species has its own habitat, food sources, predators, and behaviors. If you want to learn more about a particular species of skate or ray, put the name of the species into the search engine found on the FishBase website at www.fishbase.org. You can also visit your local library to find more books about skates, rays, and other kinds of fish.

Glossary

Note: Boldfaced words that are defined in the text may not appear in the glossary.

coral reef A large underwater structure that is made up of corals

crustaceans Ocean animals, such as crabs and lobsters, which have hard outer coverings but do not have backbones

endangered Describing animals that are in danger of disappearing from Earth forever

equator An imaginary line around the center of the Earth

fishery A company that catches fish and sells them for money

hatch To break out of an egg case

mate To join together to make babies

microscopic Describing something that is so small it can be seen only with a microscope

organ A part of the body, such as the heart, that does an important job

oxygen A gas found in air and water that animals must breathe to stay alive

pelvic fins Two fins located near the tail of a skate or a ray

polar Describing land or water that is located near the North Pole or the South Pole

population The total number of one species of animal living in an area

pupil The black part in the center of the eye, through which light passes

rain forest A hot forest that receives over 80 inches (203 cm) of rain each year

tissue A group of cells on a plant or an animal that form a thin layer

yolk The part of an egg that feeds the baby

Index

1 2 3 4 5 6 7 8 9 0 Printed in the U.S.A. 4 3 2 1 0 9 8 7 6 5